Introduction

Every major appliance we own, from our
refrigerator to our automobile, comes with an owner's
manual. Generally it's a simple, easy-to-understand booklet
which explains how the thing operates, how to program "it"
and what to do if "it" breaks down. We have all often won-
dered why our partners didn't come with an "owner's
manual."

"The Owner's Manual" is a useful little reference guide that
can tell us everything we need to know about the ones we
love, from their history to their shoe size.

Ideally, the best way to use this book is to have each partner
fill one out completely and then exchange them. We're
certain that exchanging and reading "The Owner's Manual"
will not only help you understand each other better, but you
will also discover fascinating things to talk about for a long,
long time.

This book is dedicated to Herb Tanzer.

Published by:
WonderChild Press
9250 Wilshire Blvd. #404
Beverly Hills, CA 90212
PH: 310-550-6771
FAX: 310-550-7105

Printed & bound in the United States of America

ISBN 0-9634919-1-1

Table of Contents

Table of Contents continued

History

Date of Birth _____

City_____State _____

Height_____Weight _____

Hair Color_____ Eyes _____

I am the _____child of

_____& _____

Sisters & Brothers

names_____

Significant childhood

events_____

_____

_____

_____

Favorite subjects in school_____

_____

Favorite things to do when I was little

included _____

_____

Favorite childhood toys

and/or pets _____

_____

What I wanted to be when

I grew up _____

_____

_____

_____

Favorite fairytales_____

_____

Favorite movie or TV
show_____

Kindergarten I
attended _____

_____

Elementary
School _____

_____

Jr. High _____

_____

High School _____

_____

College _____

_____

First Job I ever had_____

_____

_____

Favorite Job _____

_____

_____

Worst Job_____

_____

_____

Childhood Nicknames_____

_____

_____

The Care & Maintenance of
_____'s Body

I require _____hours of sleep per night.
If I don't get that amount this is what
happens _____

_____
I like to sleep on the _____side of the bed
and I need_____pillows,
preferably_____pillows. I like the
windows_____and the air conditioning/heater _____
If I wake up in the middle of the night
from a nightmare,
please _____

I like to take _____showers/baths per day.
This is an activity that I _____prefer to do alone.

I prefer the followings accoutrements
with my bathing_____

_____

_____

Feeding Requirements

I need to eat _____ times per day.

Preferably at _____

and _____ and _____

If I miss a meal I

get _____

My favorite breakfast foods are _____

_____

_____

My favorite lunch foods are _____

_____

_____

My favorite dinner foods are

_____

_____

_____

My favorite desserts are

_____

_____

_____

My favorite alcoholic beverages

are _____

I _____ like to cook. My specialties

include _____

_____

_____

_____

I hate the following
foods _____

I'm allergic to these
foods _____

I often crave these
foods _____

_____

Especially
when _____

My favorite restaurants

_____

_____

_____

My favorite take-out places

_____

_____

_____

My favorite meal of the day
is _____

My favorite kind of birthday cake
is _____

Pet peeves about other people's eating
habits include _____

_____

_____

_____

_____

What Makes Me, Me!

The thing that makes me different from most
people is _____
_____
_____

If I had $20 million dollars I would spend it
on _____
_____
_____
_____

I am_____interested in social change. I
really do _____believe one person can make a difference.
I think the most important social issues on the planet today
are _____
_____
_____
_____

If I were in charge, this is what I would do
about them _____
_____
_____
_____
_____

This is what I am doing _____
_____
_____
_____

The charities to which I contribute
time and/or money are _____

_____

_____

_____

If I were to be famous, this is what I would want to be famous
for _____

_____

I think the most significant differences
between men and women are _____

_____

_____

_____

The transformational/motivational seminars I
have attended are _____

_____

_____

Service organizations I belong to _____

_____

Professional organizations I belong to include _____

_____

The event that has had the most significance in
my life was _____

_____

_____

_____

The person that has had the most significance
in my life is/was _____

_____

People & things that scare me _____

_____

_____

People & things that make me laugh _____

_____

_____

The best way to get me to do something I don't
want to do is _____

_____

All of my friends come to me for _____
_____ and I _____ enjoy it.

Of all my childhood friends that I have lost contact with, the
one I would most like to see again is _____
because _____

_____

The books & movies which have shaped me
are _____

_____

_____

My phobias and superstitions are _____

_____

I was _____ years old when I left home.
I went to _____

_____

_____

My Perfect Day Would Look Like This

I would wake up at _____ The first thing that I
would do is _____
My breakfast would consist of _____
_____ After breakfast I
would then _____

_____

And after that I would _____

_____

I would eat lunch at _____o'clock and probably
have_____with _____
I would talk about _____
_____ After lunch I
would _____

_____

and then spend the rest of the day _____
_____In the early
evening I would _____
_____and then I would
have dinner at _____
with _____and
order _____

_____

After dinner I would amuse myself by_____
and go to sleep with _____
and dream about _____

_____

Alone Time

These are the things I really enjoy doing when I have time all to myself

1) _____
2) _____
3) _____
4) _____
5) _____
6) _____
7) _____
8) _____
9) _____
10) _____

Saturdays & Sundays

On Saturdays I _____ ___ _have a routine that I
_____follow.
The best time on Saturday to
surprise me is _____ and I would like
the surprise to be _____

_____

_____

_____

My idea of the perfect Saturday night is _____

_____

_____

_____

_____

On Sundays I _____have a routine that I
_____follow.
My idea of the perfect Sunday is _____

_____

_____

_____

_____

_____

Favorite Things

I like massages _____

I like to be woken up

_____

_____

I like to fall
asleep _____

_____

I need to be hugged_____times a day.

My absolute favorite thing in the world
is _____

_____

_____

_____

My idea of the perfect vacation
is _____

_____

_____

_____

_____

If I could have the world my way I
would _____

_____at least once a day.

More Favorite Things

Favorite
color _____

Favorite
gemstones _____

Favorite
flowers _____

Favorite
fragrances_____

Favorite
sounds _____

Favorite
collectibles _____

Favorite radio
station/show _____

The one thing I've never gotten that I've always
wanted _____

_____

_____

_____

_____

_____

_____

More Things

If I had come home and you had _____

_____

_____

_____

When I am at work, you _____

_____

_____

_____

Some weekend you surprise me by _____

_____

_____

_____

_____

Things I really hate are _____

_____

_____

_____

_____

_____

Upsets

I have a _____ temper.
The early warning signs that I'm angry include

_____

_____

_____

_____

_____

What to do if I'm angry with you _____

_____

_____

_____

_____

The worst possible thing to do or say when I'm
angry are _____

_____

_____

_____

I am _____moody.

Five things that will get me into a good mood

1) _____
2) _____
3) _____
4) _____
5) _____

Five things that will get me into a bad mood

1) _____
2) _____
3) _____
4) _____
5) _____

Career

Currently I earn my living doing _____
_____ What I love most
about it is _____ What frustrates
me the most about it is _____
_____

My dream for my career is to _____
_____
_____

The one thing I would most like to change about
my situation is _____
_____
_____

When I was a child, I dreamed of becoming
a _____
_____

If I had to do it all over again I would _____
_____
_____

My major accomplishments include _____
_____
_____
_____
_____

My biggest failure was _____
_____
_____

Money

I am _____ with money.

I grew up in a _____ home and the

#1 lesson I learned about money was _____

_____

_____

I _____ enjoy handling money. I currently
have the following

_____ savings account   _____ money market

_____ CDs/treasury bills   _____ safety deposit box

_____ $ under the mattress   _____ stocks & bonds

_____ IRA/Keough   _____ trust fund

other sources _____

_____

I will _____ readily loan money to a friend.

I would _____ charge interest.

I _____ know how to manuever in small claims court.

I have _____ credit cards.

I usually pay _____ each month.

Money

I _____ know my net worth. It is around _____

I wish it were _____

Money is _____ important to me. I particularly

like to use it for _____

_____

_____

_____

When asked by a transient for money I usually _____

_____

I buy Girl Scout cookies_____ I really _____

telephone solicitations. In fact they make

me _____

I _____ watch the shopping channels. I buy from

catalogues. My favorite catalogues are _____

_____

_____

I pay my bills _____

I stick to a budget _____

I balance my checkbook _____

My credit rating is _____

I _____ prefer to handle my own finances.

My outstanding debts include _____

_____

_____

_____ and total $_____

My Future

The basics I want for my life include
Marriage_____
Children_____Other_____
My favorite type of house is _____

_____

_____

_____

In 5 years I expect
to _____

_____

I plan to _____working as soon as I am
_____years old.
My other ideas for a career
include _____

_____

_____

_____

_____

If I had to do it all over again, I would
have _____

_____

_____

_____

Spiritual

I _____believe in God. My image of God
is _____As
a child, my religious upbringing was_____
_____and I _____attended
Sunday School. At the time I really_____
Today my spiritual practice includes _____

_____

_____

_____

I believe that when you die you _____

_____

_____

When I die, I would like my funeral to _____

_____

_____

_____

_____

I plan to raise my children to believe that

_____

_____

My thoughts about euthanasia are _____

_____

Daily rituals I practice are _____

_____

_____

I also do

_____Meditation   _____Angel Cards   _____Tarot

_____Yoga   _____Prayer   _____I Ching

_____Attend Mass   _____Astrology   _____Pendulum

_____A Course In Miracles   _____Read Bible

Other _____

_____

The spiritual leaders I would most like to meet
are _____

_____

_____

Relationships

The most significant romantic relationships in my life were
with _____

_____

_____

What really worked in my relationships in the past
was _____

_____

_____

_____

The former love I would most like you to get to
know is _____because _____

_____

_____

The fairytale which most influenced my thinking
about romance was _____

because_____

_____

The songs and movies which most influenced my thinking
about romance were _____

_____

_____

_____

_____

_____

Relationships

Most of my friends are _____ in a committed
relationship.

My parents are/were married for _____ years.

It was a _____ marriage. They _____
divorced. It happened when I was _____ years
old. It affected me _____

_____

_____

_____

The woman who has most influenced me in the area of
relationship was _____

The man who has most influenced me was _____

_____

My role models for committed relationships are _____

_____

_____

_____

_____

Relationships

The recurring complaints I've had about every relationship
I've been in are_____

_____

_____

_____

I can tolerate just about anything in a relationship
except_____

_____

_____

Three of the qualities my former partners loved
about me are _____

_____

_____

The lesson I have to learn in relating is _____

_____

_____

_____

My position on monogomy is _____

_____

_____

If I had a crystal ball, I would predict that in five years this
relationship will _____

_____

_____

_____

Sex

I was _____ years old the first time I made love. It was
with _____ The best part
about it was _____
_____

The worst part was _____
_____

I think the three sexiest men on the planet today
are _____
_____
_____

I think the three sexiest women on the planet today
are _____
_____
_____

Someone I've always wanted to make love with
is _____
I _____ lingerie. My favorite kind is _____
_____

The best sexual escapade I ever had was _____
_____
_____

The worst was _____
_____
_____

Sex

Favorite
positions _____

_____

Favorite
locations _____

_____

Favorite
lighting_____

_____

Favorite
music _____

_____

Something I've always wanted to try and haven't
is _____

_____

Special things I really
like _____

_____

_____

_____

_____

Erogenous
zones _____

_____

_____

_____

Sex

Favorite time of day to make
love _____

Least favorite time of day_____

Public displays of affection make
me _____

Overall I am _____affectionate.

My favorite part of my body
is _____

The part of my body I most like to have touched
is _____

I _____kissing. Particularly _____
_____

Kissing for me is like _____

My ideal partner would like to have sex _____times
a _____ And, it would take
as long as _____

Sometimes I _____a quickie.

I would describe my orgasms as _____
_____
_____

Immediately after orgasm I need you to _____
_____
_____

Sex

I am most in the mood for sex_____

_____

_____

Making love during menstruation_____

_____

After making love I like to eat _____

_____

Sex toys I enjoy are _____

My favorite store to buy oils, lotions & potions

is _____

The kinkiest thing I have ever done is _____

_____

During sex I am   _____Noisy   _____Quiet

_____Animated _____Seductive _____Kinky

_____Silly   _____Animal-like_____Macho

_____Talkative _____ Other _____

In the area of sex _____

_____

pushes me over the edge. I _____dirty talk. I _____
enjoy sex with more than one partner. If I knew someone
was watching, I would _____

The type of sex that really turns me off is _____

_____

The most intimate sexual experience anyone has ever shared
with me is_____

_____

Romance

I consider myself to be_____romantic.

My favorite time of day for romance is _____
_____

My idea of a romantic encounter is _____

_____

_____

_____

_____

_____

One of my fantasies for a romantic night is

to _____

_____

_____

_____

_____

I think the most romantic place in the world is

_____

_____

_____

_____

Romance

The music that puts me in a romantic
mood is _____

_____

_____

The movies that put me in a romantic
mood are _____

_____

_____

The following things put a damper on
romance _____

_____

_____

My idea of a very romantic gift is _____

_____

_____

The worst gift I ever received from anyone
was _____

_____

Romance is a _____priority in my life. The
most romantic thing anyone has ever done for
me _____

_____

_____

_____

_____

Romance

The following days/holidays are very important romantic
days for me _____

_____

When I ask for romance, what I really want
is _____

_____

_____

_____

_____

_____

_____

_____

Fantasies

I have always wanted to "do it" in the following places _____

_____

_____

_____

_____

_____

_____

My top three sexual fantasies include _____

_____

_____

_____

_____

_____

_____

_____

_____

_____

_____

Dates

My idea of a great date is to
Rent a video
comedy_____action_____drama_____x _____
(and stay in with popcorn)
Go out to dinner   alone_____with friends_____
Go to the movies _____
Go to the drive-in _____
Go to the theatre_____ Picnic_____
Museums_____Concerts_____
Dancing
_____ Square _____ Tango/Salsa_____ Disco
_____ Ballroom _____ Two-step
_____ Other_____
Ball Games_____ to see _____
_____
Bowling_____ Shopping_____
Gambling _____ Bingo _____
Other _____
_____
_____
_____
_____

Vacations

My dream vacation would
include _____

_____

_____

_____

_____

_____

_____

_____

Places I want to see before I
die _____

_____

_____

_____

_____

_____

_____

_____

_____

Types of Vacations I Prefer

tropical islands_____ wilderness_____
camping_____ 5-star hotels_____
spontaneous_____ car trips_____
rafting/adventure_____ancient ruins_____
high-tech_____ group tours_____
family fun_____ gambling_____
anything by bus_____ by train_____
Australia_____ Acapulco_____Athens_____
Aspen_____ Bangkok_____ Brazil_____
Bali_____ Canada_____Cairo_____
Caribbean_____ Denmark_____ Dallas_____
Ethiopia_____ England_____ Finland_____
France_____ Germany_____ Hawaii_____
Italy_____ Ireland_____ Istanbul_____
Jamaica_____ Japan_____ Jakarta_____
Kenya_____ Lima_____ Monterey_____
Madrid_____ Nepal_____ New Zealand_____
New Orleans_____ Ottawa_____ Paris_____
Quebec_____ Rio_____Singapore_____
San Juan_____ St. Barts_____ Sweden_____
South America_____ Tahiti_____ Tangier_____
Tasmania_____Venezuela_____Yellowstone_____
Other _____

_____

_____

Holidays

I like to spend New Year's Eve _____

_____

_____

_____

_____

For Valentine's Day I would
love _____

_____

_____

_____

I like to spend Easter/Passover_____

_____

_____

_____

My idea of a great Mother's Day is _____

_____

_____

_____

_____

Holidays

Memorial Day Weekend is a great time to _____

_____

_____

_____

My idea of great Father's Day is _____

_____

_____

Fourth of July should be spent _____

_____

_____

Labor Day is best spent _____

_____

_____

Halloween _____
Thanksgiving _____

_____

Christmas is best spent _____

_____

_____

My fantasy birthday celebration consists of_____

_____

_____

_____

_____

Sports & Leisure Activities

My favorite sports to participate in are _____
_____
_____
_____

My favorite sports to watch are _____
_____
_____

My favorite leisure acitivies are _____
_____
_____
_____

My idea of heaven on a Saturday or Sunday
afternoon is to _____
_____
_____
_____

The activity I am best at is _____
_____
_____
_____
_____

Shopping

I_____shopping. In fact I would spend_____time
shopping, if I could.
My favorite stores to shop in are _____

_____

_____

_____

_____

My sizes are
Dress/Suit_____Blouse/Shirt_____
Shoe_____Ring_____Socks/Pantyhose_____
Underwear_____Bathing suit_____Pants_____
Hat_____
Favorite colors for
clothes _____

I like clothes that
are _____

Favorite designers _____

_____

Fabrics I love _____

_____

Fabrics I hate _____

_____

Music & Movies

My musical abilities consist of _____

_____

My favorite musicians are _____

_____

_____

_____

The best concert I ever went to was _____

_____

Someday I would like to see_____

_____

_____

My all-time favorite movies_____

_____

_____

_____

_____

I like_____movies best and please don't take
me to any_____movies.
I like my popcorn _____ My favorite theatre is

_____

My favorite movie stars are _____

_____

_____

_____

_____

Television

I watch television _____
My favorite TV shows are _____

_____

_____

_____

_____

I like to watch TV in the _____room & I like to
eat _____while I'm
watching TV.
Being in control of the remote control is_____
important to me. In fact _____

_____
I _____fall asleep with the TV on.
In the morning I _____watch TV. My favorite morning
show is _____
I really like it because_____

_____

_____

My favorite talk show host is _____
My least favorite talk show host is _____
In my fantasies, I would love to be a talk show host
just like _____

Friends

My very best friend
is _____

Some of my favorite friends
are _____

_____

_____

Things I like to do with my friends _____

_____

_____

_____

When you can't figure out what to do with me or what to get
for me, please call _____

at (_____) _____

I think these qualities are very important in
a friend_____

_____

_____

_____

_____

_____

_____

_____

_____

Transportation

Generally I _____ driving.

My dream car is a_____

I learned how to drive when I was_____ years old.

_____ taught me how. It

was a _____ experience.

My favorite form of travel is by

airplane_____ train_____ boat_____ bus_____

helicopter_____ other _____

If I were very rich, I would own

a _____

When I'm in heavy traffic, I generally

get _____

I consider my traffic record to be

Above average_____ Average_____

Below Average_____ Terrible_____

Health

I am _____ healthy. To stay healthy

I eat _____

I exercise _____

The only health problems I have consist of _____

_____

_____

_____

The medications I must take are _____

_____

_____

Something you should know about my health

is _____

_____

_____

_____

My family has a history of _____

_____

_____

I expect to live to age_____

Health

I have had the following illnesses

_____colds_____flu_____virus

_____measles _____mumps _____chicken pox

_____cold sores _____mono_____STDs

_____heart attack

Others _____

_____

_____

_____

_____

I have _____been admitted to a hospital. It was

in_____for _____

My health insurance carrier is _____

_____

I take _____care of my health.

When I get sick it is usually because of _____

_____

_____

_____

_____

Animals & Books

My favorite pet is _____

The first animal I ever owned was

a _____

I am allergic to _____

In fact, if I even get near a _____, I

get _____

Ideally, I would like to have_____pets. They

would include _____

_____

The best book I ever read

was _____

My favorite authors

are _____

_____

_____

_____

My favorite time to read is_____

I _____loan out my books. If I don't get them

back I _____

_____

Family

Today my family consists of
Wife/Husband _____
Children (& ages) _____

_____

_____

Ex's _____
Sisters _____

_____

Brothers _____

_____

Parents _____
Grandparents _____
Aunts & Uncles _____

_____

_____

Cousins _____

_____

Others _____

_____

I am _____ close to my family. My favorite
is _____
because _____

_____

_____

_____

Things That Would Really Make Me Happy and Sad

If I came home and you had _____

_____

_____

When I am at work you _____

_____

_____

Some weekend you surprised me by _____

_____

_____

_____

Things I really hate _____

_____

_____

_____

Things that make me cry _____

_____

_____

_____

_____

_____

In Case of Emergency

Please contact _____

Home phone _____

Office phone _____

Office friends' names _____

_____

My doctors are

Medical _____ Ph.(____)_____

Dentist _____ Ph.(____)_____

Veterinarian _____ Ph.(____)_____

Chiropractor _____ Ph.(____)_____

Other Doctors _____ Ph.(____)_____

Misc #'s

Hairdresser _____ Ph.(____)_____

Manicurist _____ Ph.(____)_____

Masseuse _____ Ph.(____)_____

Others _____ Ph.(____)_____

_____ Ph.(____)_____

_____ Ph.(____)_____

_____ Ph.(____)_____

_____ Ph.(____)_____

_____ Ph.(____)_____

© 1992
WonderChild Press   310/550-6771
9250 Wilshire Blvd., #404, Beverly Hills, CA 90212